A *LifeGuide*® Bible Study

*G*OD'S LOVE
Knowing God Through the Psalms

10 studies for individuals or groups

Ruth Ann Ridley

With Notes for Leaders

InterVarsity Press
Downers Grove, Illinois

InterVarsity Press
P.O. Box 1400, Downers Grove, IL 60515-1426
World Wide Web: www.ivpress.com
E-mail: mail@ivpress.com

InterVarsity Press® is the book-publishing division of InterVarsity Christian Fellowship/USA®, a student movement active on campus at hundreds of universities, colleges and schools of nursing in the United States of America, and a member movement of the International Fellowship of Evangelical Students. For information about local and regional activities, write Public Relations Dept., InterVarsity Christian Fellowship/USA, 6400 Schroeder Rd., P.O. Box 7895, Madison, WI 53707-7895, or visit the IVCF website at <www.ivcf.org>.

LifeGuide® is a registered trademark of InterVarsity Christian Fellowship.

Cover image: Beverly Joubert/National Geographic Image Collection

ISBN 0-8308-3085-5

Printed in the United States of America ∞

P	17	16	15	14	13	12	11	10	9	8	7	6	5	4	3	2
Y	17	16	15	14	13	12	11	10	09	08	07	06	05	04		

Contents

Getting the Most Out of
God's Love

Do you ever wish you could get away from yourself? The Christian philosopher Søren Kierkegaard did. "Death and [cursing]!" he said, "I can disassociate from everything else but my own self; I can't even forget myself when I am asleep" (*The Diary of Søren Kierkegaard*). Sometimes it's essential that we analyze ourselves, search out the places we err and understand the reasons we do what we do. But too much self-searching can lead to torment.

David was a man after God's own heart and the principal author of the psalms. Like Kierkegaard, David was a man who searched himself. In the record the Bible gives us of the history and longings of this man, we see what it means to be human. There was sin in David's life, and there was doubt. But in every circumstance he dealt with God. He kept bending his inner analysis upward, finishing with a searching out of the nature of God. And there he found health.

Romans 8:6 says, "Obsession with self . . . is a dead end; attention to God leads us out into the open, into a spacious, free life" (*The Message*). The question "Who is God?" is a question that can occupy our whole lives. It leads us to ask other questions such as those Henri Nouwen asks in *Genesee Diary:* "Why is the Lord of justice also the Lord of Love; the God of fear, also the God of gentle compassion?"

The psalms touch on many such questions and then go on to ask the question "What shall we do because of who we discover God to be?" In this priceless book of questioning and praising, certain aspects of God's nature recur over and over again. He is Creator, Helper, Lover and King, and because this is who he is, he satisfies, understands, calms fears, restores, strengthens, listens, gives refuge and reigns. His love for each of us is so vast and all-covering that we wrestle to even begin to believe it. His kingship manifests itself in victories and wisdoms too many to count. He is splendid, but unlike earthly kings, his thoughts are not wrapped up in his splendor. They are wrapped up in those he loves.

"You're my friend and you're my brother," writes Martin Nystrom, "even though you are a King" ("As the Deer"). In another verse Nystrom writes, "We long to worship Thee." I like the humility of that sentence. Who knows, really, how to worship God? All we can do is turn our thoughts toward him, observe how his greatest servants worshiped him and make an effort at our own praise. That's what this guide is for.

Along with the inductive Bible studies, there are some special features in this guide: each study has a song that expands the theme of the study and has ideas for creating a worship journal (see the leader's notes for study 1 for ideas on using these). My prayer is that these tools will help us learn to worship, to think on the One who loves us and forever deserves our praise.

Suggestions for Individual Study

1. As you begin each study, pray that God will speak to you through his Word.

2. Read the introduction to the study and respond to the personal reflection question or exercise. This is designed to help you focus on God and on the theme of the study.

3. Each study deals with a particular passage—so that you can delve into the author's meaning in that context. Read and reread the passage to be studied. The questions are written using the language of the New International Version, so you may wish to use that version of the Bible. The New Revised Standard Version is also recommended.

4. This is an inductive Bible study, designed to help you discover for yourself what Scripture is saying. The study includes three types of questions. *Observation* questions ask about the basic facts: who, what, when, where and how. *Interpretation* questions delve into the meaning of the passage. *Application* questions help you discover the implications of the text for growing in Christ. These three keys unlock the treasures of Scripture.

Write your answers to the questions in the spaces provided or in a personal journal. Writing can bring clarity and deeper understanding of yourself and of God's Word.

5. It might be good to have a Bible dictionary handy. Use it to look up any unfamiliar words, names or places.

6. Use the prayer suggestion to guide you in thanking God for what you have learned and to pray about the applications that have come to mind.

7. You may want to go on to the suggestion under "Now or Later," or you may want to use that idea for your next study.

Suggestions for Members of a Group Study

1. Come to the study prepared. Follow the suggestions for individual study mentioned above. You will find that careful preparation will greatly enrich your time spent in group discussion.

2. Be willing to participate in the discussion. The leader of your group will not be lecturing. Instead, he or she will be encouraging the members of the group to discuss what they have learned. The leader will be asking the questions that are found in this guide.

3. Stick to the topic being discussed. Your answers should be based on the verses which are the focus of the discussion and not on outside authorities such as commentaries or speakers. These studies focus on a particular passage of Scripture. Only rarely should you refer to other portions of the Bible. This allows for everyone to participate in indepth study on equal ground.

4. Be sensitive to the other members of the group. Listen attentively when they describe what they have learned. You may be surprised by their insights! Each question assumes a variety of answers. Many questions do not have "right" answers, particularly questions that aim at meaning or application. Instead the questions push us to explore the passage more thoroughly.

When possible, link what you say to the comments of others. Also, be affirming whenever you can. This will encourage some of the more hesitant members of the group to participate.

5. Be careful not to dominate the discussion. We are sometimes so eager to express our thoughts that we leave too little opportunity for others to respond. By all means participate! But allow others to also.

6. Expect God to teach you through the passage being discussed and through the other members of the group. Pray that you will have an enjoyable and profitable time together, but also that as a result of the study you will find ways that you can take action individually and/or as a group.

7. Remember that anything said in the group is considered confidential and should not be discussed outside the group unless specific permission is given to do so.

8. If you are the group leader, you will find additional suggestions at the back of the guide.

1

The God
Who Satisfies

Psalm 104

When you open your hand,
they are satisfied with good things.
PSALM 104:28

What is there about nature that allures and soothes so completely? Aching inside, I drive along a trafficked street and come upon a park that autumn has turned into a fairyland: reds, oranges and tree-fields smothered in burnished gold. My mood lifts, comforted at such beauty from the hand of a God who cares.

The desire of the Creator is to give his people soul satisfaction. How full of desires we are! How those desires can plague us when they are unfulfilled! As T. S. Eliot said, "Desire itself is movement, not in itself desirable" (*Four Quartets*). Yet we live constantly thirsty for love, for things, for answers, for "more."

GROUP DISCUSSION. What do you particularly enjoy in nature, and why?

PERSONAL REFLECTION. What kinds of incidents or situations sometimes cause you to feel the need for something more?

God is the ultimate source of thirst quenching. The more we focus on him, the more satisfaction we will experience. In Psalm 104 David meditates on nature to learn more about God. The result is praise. *Read Psalm 104.*

---

1. What themes do you see in this psalm?

Which of these do you particularly resonate with?

---

2. In verses 1-4 David soars in a poetic description of God's greatness. What everyday images does David use to help us begin to understand God's splendor and power?

---

3. What do you learn about God from verses 5-9?

---

4. How has God shown his power or his benevolent control in your life? (Think of help that seemed providential, answers to prayer, provision in an intense time of need and so on.)

---

5. Remembering that the Psalms are poems and almost always have more than one meaning, what universal needs do the following verses show God meets?
Verses 10-16:

Verses 17-18:

Verses 19-26:

---

6. Psalm 104 shows that the creation is dependent on God. Why do you think it is difficult for us to remember our own dependence on God?

---

7. Verses 27-30 form a key passage in Psalm 104. It contains summaries and conclusions of what has come before. What is God doing for humanity as part of his creation?

---

8. What does it mean to be satisfied?

---

9. Reread verses 31-35. How would you like to trust God for provision or satisfaction in your life right now? Express what you are most in need of today: security, order, variety, renewal, hope, something more basic.

With a sense of expectation, offer your specific needs to God in prayer.

Now or Later

Responding with Praise. Read or sing the following hymn.

As the Deer

As the deer panteth for the water, so my soul longeth after Thee.
You alone are my heart's desire, and I long to worship Thee.

You alone are my strength, my shield;
To You alone may my spirit yield.

You alone are my heart's desire, and I long to worship Thee.

I want You more than gold or silver, only You can satisfy.
You alone are the real joy giver and the apple of my eye.

You alone are my strength, my shield;
To You alone may my spirit yield.

You alone are my heart's desire, and I long to worship Thee.

Worship Journal. In a separate notebook begin a worship journal for deeper meditation. To probe the spiritual meanings of Psalm 104's allusions to water, read the passage on living water in John 4:7-13. Record thoughts and questions. If you enjoy working with images, draw or tape a picture of an abundant source of water, for example a waterfall or a spring, beneath your meditations.

2

The God
Who Understands

Great is our Lord, and of great power:
his understanding is infinite.
PSALM 147:5 KJV

Praise isn't natural. There are so many needs in our own lives and in those around us that it's easier to be frantic than to be hopeful. Yet God says that he inhabits the praises of his people, that he becomes more real to us when we praise.

Perhaps we could learn from Mozart who, though fallible, was given a talent by God that has blessed us for centuries. Karl Barth says that in Mozart's music "there is a turning in which the light rises and the shadows fall, though without disappearing, in which joy overtakes sorrow without extinguishing it, in which the Yea rings louder than the ever-present Nay" (*Wolfgang Amadeus Mozart*).

GROUP DISCUSSION. What are some reasons for praise in your life or in the world as you perceive it today? (Start small and see how many things you can name.)

PERSONAL REFLECTION. What is happening in your life right now that makes you feel frantic or depressed? What is giving you hope?

God doesn't ask us to be blind to the shadows. But he does urge us to be alert to the ever-present reasons for praise. And he probes the hearts of his people every day, empathizing. He understands the great and ringing name of every star. God's magnitude is far beyond our imagination. Yet he is passionately interested in you and me. *Read Psalm 147.*

---

1. This is a psalm of pure praise. Notice the present-tense verbs that show what God is doing now. Which of these would you most like to see God doing in your life?

---

2. We can praise God for what surrounds us as well as for what is within us. What inner things is the psalmist praising God for?

---

3. What people does God show a special interest in (vv. 2-3, 6)?

Contrast these people with the types of people our culture tends to exalt or admire.

---

4. Review verses 1-6. God understands everything! What act of God's understanding love in these verses speaks to you? Why?

---

5. Read verses 7-11. Here the psalmist intensifies his praise, singing with thanksgiving and making music on the harp. Why do you think he is thanking God for the insight of verses 10-11?

6. Why do you think it is difficult for most of us to put our "hope in his unfailing love" (v. 11)?

---

7. Verses 12-14 speak of the way God helps his nation. In your own words write what you think the psalmist might mean for a nation or for an individual when he says, "He strengthens the bars of your gates" (v. 13)?

---

8. What do you learn about God's spoken and written word in verses 15-20?

---

9. Compare the effect of our words to the effect of God's. What is the significance of the phrase "His word runs swiftly" (v. 15)?

---

10. God understands all your confusions and hurts. With just a word, he could answer your prayers or change the cosmos. Where would you like God to use his infinite insight to help you in your life today? (Consider possible needs such as: the need for sorting out confusion, for wisdom about a decision, discernment about problems in a relationship or relief from feelings of alienation.)

Offer your praise to the God who understands us better than we understand ourselves.

Now or Later

Responding with Praise. Read or sing the following hymn.

All Creatures of Our God and King

All creatures of our God and King,
Lift up your voice and with us sing,
Alleluia, Alleluia! Thou burning sun with golden beam,
Thou silver moon with softer gleam,
O praise Him, O praise Him,
Alleluia, alleluia, alleluia!

Thou rushing wind that art so strong,
Ye clouds that sail in heav'n along,
O praise Him, Alleluia! Thou rising morn in praise rejoice,
Ye lights of evening, find a voice,
O praise Him, O praise Him,
Alleluia, alleluia, alleluia!

Let all things their Creator bless,
And worship Him in humbleness,
O praise Him, Alleluia!
Praise, praise the Father, praise the Son,
And praise the Spirit three in one,
O praise Him, O praise Him,
Alleluia, alleluia, alleluia!

Text by St. Francis of Assisi, English translation by William Draper ©1923 (renewed)
by J. Curwen and Sons, Ltd. All rights for U.S. and Canada controlled by G. Schirmer,
Inc. Reprinted by permission.

Worship Journal. Choose one of the following prayer-thoughts: (1)
Lord, I want to delight in you. Show me how. (2) I praise you, Father,
that even though I may not understand the "why" of something right
now, I can trust you to be loving and faithful toward me in all you do.
In your journal, enlarge the prayer you chose. Add specifics about
your circumstances. Explore ways God has been gentle and understanding with you.

3

The God Who Helps

Psalm 40

O LORD, come quickly to help me.
PSALM 40:13

We've all experienced times when we've analyzed a problem until we can analyze it no more, done all we can do and possess no more resources. To struggle alone any longer becomes intolerable. In these moments we call out, "God help me!"—the most common prayer in the world and the most underrated. When we ask God to help us, it is like asking a sensitive, loving friend for relief, but this friend possesses infinite foresight and ability.

GROUP DISCUSSION. When we help someone, we lift a load or provide a remedy. In what areas do you sometimes feel overwhelmed and wish for this kind of help?

PERSONAL REFLECTION. List the dilemmas you've faced during this last year. Which problems still linger despite all your efforts to resolve them?

Sometimes even when we plead for God's help, he doesn't come. In Psalm 40 we find David flailing. He speaks with honesty about his anger and helplessness. He seeks a larger perspective. Then he waits for God to help at the proper time. *Read Psalm 40.*

1. What past, present and future attitudes and situations does the psalmist refer to?

2. Look again at verses 1-4. Picture yourself falling into a deep pit with slimy walls. How would you feel, and what would you do?

3. Why do you think he uses the analogies of mud and mire, then a rock and a firm place to describe some of life's situations?

4. What portion of verse 5 particularly stands out to you, and why?

5. Righteousness (or goodness) is a key theme in verses 6-10. Why might sacrifices and offerings be something God doesn't want?

6. *Read Hebrews 10:3-7, 10.* What new meanings does this passage add to David's psalm?

7. Return to Psalm 40. What do verses 6-10 reveal about David's relationship with God?

_____

8. What is David saying about true righteousness (vv. 6, 8-10, 12)?

_____

9. Compare the innumerable things in verse 12 and the innumerable things in verse 5. What wisdom can you glean from the comparison?

_____

10. What six things does David pray for in verses 13-16?

_____

11. David realized he needed God's help even to desire to do the right thing (vv. 10, 12). Consider your strengths and weaknesses and ways you would like to be a better person. Where would you like God's help?

_____

12. Verse 17 is a summary of the main themes in this psalm. Survey the chapter to find a phrase that means the most to you today. What would you like to do about it? (This could be anything from asking God for help in some situation to sharing something you've learned with a friend.)

Ask Jesus to open your eyes so you can see what actions he's taking in your life.

Now or Later

Responding with Praise. Read or sing the following hymn.

Bless His Holy Name

Bless the Lord,
O my soul, and all that is within me,
Bless His holy Name.
Bless the Lord,
O my soul, and all that is within me,
Bless His holy Name.

He has done great things,
He has done great things,
He has done great things,
Bless His holy name.

Bless the Lord,
O my soul, and all that is within me,
Bless His holy name.

©1973 Andrae Crouch, Bud John Songs, Inc. All rights administered by EMI Christian Music Publishing. Used by permission.

Worship Journal. God is involved intimately with us. His thoughts about each of us are as many and as varied as the leaves of a forest. Reread Psalm 40 in a different translation, maybe a contemporary version like *The Message* or the New Living Translation. Note your favorite phrases. Choose two to write out in your own words. Don't be afraid to paraphrase freely. This is your honest seeking to grasp the truth of God's help for your own life.

4

The God Who Calms Fears

*Though an army besiege me,
my heart will not fear.*
PSALM 27:3

Imagine what it would be like to live a life with no fears: never dreading a confrontation, never worrying about money, never being afraid of missing a plane or not getting everything done! What would it be like to rest in a place where we never experienced anxiety over our weaknesses or feared a doctor's findings or an accident on the highway?

In *Whistling in the Dark* Frederich Buechner says that telling a human being not to worry is "like telling a woman with a bad head cold not to sniffle and sneeze so much or a lame man to stop dragging his feet. Or maybe it is more like telling . . . a compulsive gambler to stay away from the track." Most of us are addicted to worry.

GROUP DISCUSSION. Our age has been called the "Age of Anxiety." What aspects of twenty-first-century living cause many to be plagued by anxious thoughts?

PERSONAL REFLECTION. Some people are more prone to anxiety than others. Where would you rate yourself on a scale of one to ten (one meaning you seldom worry and ten you constantly worry)? What kinds of events or expectations tend to make you anxious?

In Psalm 27 David recounts his worries, twisting and recurring like ours, but he also reminds himself of the championing of his God. He shows us that the more we understand what God is for us today, the more we'll live with courage instead of fear. *Read Psalm 27.*

1. What do we learn about David's relationship to God in this psalm? Consider his fears and desires.

2. Reread verses 1-3. What does light do, and how is God like light?

3. Study verses 5 and 10, then look again at verses 1-3. How is God a stronghold (or shelter) for us?

4. What forces (or enemies) today can consume, use or injure us?

5. What is David expecting to happen as a result of seeking God?

6. God is an omnipotent, omnipresent God, but each of us experiences the reality of his presence more at certain times than we do others. When and where do you feel God's presence the most?

---

7. In verses 7 12 we have David's very human prayer about his current situation. We can use it as a pattern for prayers about our worries. Create a title or theme that summarizes each verse.

Verse 7:

Verse 8:

Verse 9:

Verse 10:

Verse 11:

Verse 12:

---

8. What aspects of David's prayer challenge you about your own approach to prayer?

How?

---

9. Restate verse 13 in your own words, making it as personal as possible.

---

10. Reread verse 14. Why does it take courage to wait? (Think about a specific wait in your own life.)

11. When has God helped you by guiding you or giving you some kind of shelter when you were fearful?

Ask God to help you trust him with your fears, to be your deliverer.

Now or Later

Responding with Praise. Read or sing the following hymn.

A Mighty Fortress Is Our God

And though this world, with devils filled,
Should threaten to undo us,
We will not fear, for God hath willed
His truth to triumph through us:
The Prince of Darkness grim,
We tremble not for him;
His rage we can endure,
For lo, his doom is sure;
One little word shall fell him.

Martin Luther

Worship Journal. Spend time praying a "casting-care prayer." (1) Make a list of all of your fears and worries, small and large. (2) Pray each item on your list back to God, taking time to talk to him about all aspects of each fear. Pray until you feel you've truly left your worries with God.

Copy the following for future memory: "Don't fret or worry. Instead of worrying, pray. Let petitions and praises shape your worries into prayers, letting God know your concerns. Before you know it, a sense of God's wholeness, everything coming together for good, will come and settle you down. It's wonderful what happens when Christ displaces worry at the center of your life" (Philippians 4:6-7 *The Message*).

5

The God
Who Restores

Weeping may remain for a night,
but rejoicing comes in the morning.
PSALM 30:5

Our lives are lived in cycles. We fall. We plead for help and receive it. We run well, and then we fall again. We plead. God lifts us up. We hope and try, and soon we've tumbled again. Experiences of illness and health, failure and success, loss and restoration are part of being human.

GROUP DISCUSSION. What examples of illness followed by health or failure followed by success have you seen in other believer's lives or experienced in your own?

PERSONAL REFLECTION. Do you lean more toward relying on your own competence or relying on God's mercy? Write about a recent incident when you did one or the other.

By the time David wrote this psalm he had faced Goliath, escaped Saul's javelin, lost his best friend, alienated his own followers and succumbed to the temptation of pride. Over and over again he had to be reminded that it was not because of his merit that God came to his rescue, but because of God's mercy alone. David knew the habit of reviewing answers to prayer in the past could be a source of strength and hope in the present. He wrote Psalm 30 for a day of dedication. The song is a summary of many restorations. *Read Psalm 30.*

1. List the strong, active verbs in this passage.

What do they show about why David is praising God?

2. David probably wrote this psalm for the dedication of his palace, described in 2 Samuel 5:6-12. How do these events set the stage for this psalm?

3. Return to Psalm 30. In verses 1-3 David lifts God up. How does David see himself?

4. In Hebrew the word *heal* can also mean "to freshen, to purify, or to take care" (*New American Standard Exhaustive Concordance of the Bible*). It carries the idea of restoration. Tell about a time when you needed some kind of restoration (physical, emotional, spiritual).

5. What contrasts do you see in verses 4-5?

_____

6. What past abundances or answered prayers would you like to praise God for today?

_____

7. What do you picture when you think of the anger of God (v. 5)?

How is God's anger different from our anger?

_____

8. Hebrew poetry uses parallelism or "thought rhythm." The sense of a word or phrase in one clause is more fully set forth in the following clause. How does verse 7 help you understand David's dangerous attitude in verse 6?

_____

9. List strong, emphatic words in verses 8-10 that describe David's state and God's character.

_____

10. What do the questions in verse 9 reveal about David's heart?

11. Compare verses 11 and 12 with verse 5. What assurance do you receive for your own life from these verses?

12. Thinking we can earn God's favor can fling us into a prideful mode of living that God despises. He would rather we admit our need as human beings and rely on him as God. In what area of your life do you need to rely more on his mercy?

Ask God to help you depend on his mercy today and every day of your life.

Now or Later

Responding with Praise. Read or sing the following hymn.

The Steadfast Love of the Lord

The steadfast love of the Lord never ceases.
His mercies never come to an end.
They are new every morning, new every morning.
Great is thy faithfulness, O Lord.
Great is thy faithfulness.

By Edith McNeill copyright ©1974 Celebration (Administered by The Copyright Company, Nashville, TN). Used by permission.

Worship Journal. George MacDonald said, "Fold the arms of faith and wait for the light to arise in the darkness" (as quoted in Bob and Michael Benson, *Disciplines for the Inner Life*). Morning has long symbolized new light or new hope. Spend some time writing your thoughts on morning. Include a drawing if you like.

6

The God
Who Strengthens

Psalm 18:1-36

*It is God who arms me with strength
and makes my way perfect.*
PSALM 18:32

In Psalm 18:19 David says God brought him into a "spacious place."
Reading this, I think of being given room to maneuver, room to
breathe. I see myself cut loose from the noose of fear and infused with
confidence to move forward. I think of being given strength to think
and act.

When David tells about the strength he has wielded over his enemies, he crows like a child. He boasts about how his foes have been
forced to make room for him. But after each boast, he quickly throws
the credit back to God.

GROUP DISCUSSION. What do you think it means to be a strong person?

PERSONAL REFLECTION. Make a list of your strengths. Then write
about some areas where you feel a need for growth, where you feel
fragile, powerless or weak.

David knew his strengths, and they were great; but he also knew his weaknesses. He understood his need for the power of God. *Read Psalm 18:1-36.*

1. Note all the verses that refer to some kind of strength. How does this picture of the Lord's strength give you hope?

2. Note the phrases that include the word *my* in verses 1-3. What does it reveal about this psalm?

3. What do verses 3 and 6 teach about how we can seek refuge in God?

What other ways do you think of?

4. In verses 4-5 David depicts himself as being bound hand and foot. He is facing a challenge for which he has no more resources. Have you ever faced such a challenge? Explain.

5. Verses 7-19 is a poetic description of how God intervened for David in desperate situations. What images show God's power?

6. Reread verses 20-25. What are some of the habits or characteristics of David's life that show integrity?

7. Psalm 18:19 says God rescued David because he delighted in him. How does God manifest his delight in David according to verses 24-25?

In what areas do you think he delights in you?

8. The word *blameless* in verse 23 is better translated "complete" or "having integrity." God will be faithful to strengthen us if our heart's desire is to walk in the direction of his tread. In what area of your life would you like to follow God more closely this week?

9. In verse 26 David is saying that those who walk contrary to God will experience the consequences of their sin. What principles do verses 27-36 offer for how we can stay close to God?

10. In verse 34 David says God "trains my hands for battle." We will be able to trust God more if we recognize the way he trains us ahead of time for life's difficulties. How has God prepared you for a spiritual, vocational, practical or relational challenge?

11. What kind of strength do you need in your life right now?

Pray about your needs for strength, and thank God that he will intervene.

Now or Later

Responding with Praise. Read or sing the following hymn.

A Mighty Fortress

Did we in our own strength confide,
Our striving would be losing,
Were not the right Man on our side,
The man of God's own choosing:
Dost ask who that may be?
Christ Jesus, it is He;
Lord Sabaoth His name,
From age to age the same,
And He must win the battle.

Martin Luther

Worship Journal. Consider Psalm 18:28-29. Contrast it with Proverbs 21:4. What kinds of light does a proud person have? a godly person? Write a prayer about light and strength.

7

The God Who Listens

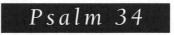

Psalm 34

The eyes of the LORD *are on the righteous*
and his ears are attentive to their cry.
PSALM 34:15

The method God has chosen for bestowing the goodness of his atten-tiveness on us is relationship. We talk and he listens. He asks and we answer. We speak and he responds, steadying us and giving us more of himself. He is near to each of us, always listening and longing for us to do the same.

GROUP DISCUSSION. Describe what you do when you are seeking to be attentive to someone. (Or describe what a relative or friend does for you when they are being especially attentive.)

PERSONAL REFLECTION. Choose one or two phrases that best express your relationship to God at this stage of your life: questioning him, praising him, asking him for things, sitting still until I hear him speak, trying to find him, asking for his guidance throughout my day, telling him how angry I am at him, waiting on him, talking *at* him. Talk with God about how you've related to him this way during the last week.

The results of God's attentiveness to us are in the promises in Psalm 34, and they are extravagant. Can we believe them? They are as extravagantly good as God himself. The psalmist urges us to taste for ourselves and see: Didn't I tell you? God is good! *Read Psalm 34.*

1. List all references to speaking and listening.

What does this tell you about the relationship between God and David?

—————————————————————————————————

2. What words would you use to describe the mood of verses 1-3?

—————————————————————————————————

3. The term *glorify* in verse 3 is sometimes translated "magnify." What happens when you use a magnifying glass to examine a butterfly or a fine print?

How does genuine worship accomplish something similar in our relationship to God?

—————————————————————————————————

4. What was God's response to David's seeking and calling in verses 4-7? Put it in your own words.

—————————————————————————————————

5. Seeking God (vv. 4, 10, 14) is something like going on a quest. Your intent is serious, your goal specific. You might be searching until you are sure of his counsel. Or you might be waiting to sense his presence in an extended time of meditation. What do you need to seek God for at this time in your life?

6. Read verses 8-10. How does the parallelism of verse 10 clarify verse 9?

What does the first part of verse 10 imply about some specific needs God promises to meet?

7. Those who seek to make God central in their lives are often described as "fearing the Lord." According to verses 11-16, what are some of the outward evidences that a person fears (or reverences) God?

8. Why does David begin his lesson with the use of the tongue (v. 13)?

9. Consider the state of your relationships. Where might God be asking you to use your tongue to make peace (v. 14)?

10. Why do you think God may be especially attentive to the broken-hearted (vv. 17-18)?

11. Do you believe God listens to you? Why or why not?

12. Choose a promise from Psalm 34 that is especially meaningful to you. Copy it below. How does it speak to you today?

You may want to memorize this promise so you can continue to claim it until you realize God has heard and is beginning to answer.

God wants to relate to you all day, back and forth, in the manner of an intimate friend. Ask him to help you to be silent more often so you can hear him speak.

Now or Later

Responding with Praise. Read or sing the following hymn.

As the Deer

You're my friend and You are my brother
even though You are a king.
I love You more than any other,
So much more than anything.
You alone are my strength, my shield;
To You alone may my spirit yield.
You alone are my heart's desire,
and I long to worship Thee.

By Martin Nystrom copyright ©1984 Maranatha! Music (Administered by The Copyright Company, Nashville, TN). Used by permission.

Worship Journal. When we are long and steadfast in our contemplation of God, he will respond to us, and we will reflect his glory. Study your calendar and carve out a morning (or another space of time) for spending two or three hours in a quiet place with God. Plan to include reading the Word, praying, praising and listening. Record the date and place and the helps you will use (your worship journal? a list of the promises you are claiming? a different translation of the Bible? a devotional book?).

8

The God
Who Gives Refuge

Psalm 31

*In the shelter of your presence you hide them
from human plots;
you hold them safe under your shelter
from contentious tongues.*
PSALM 31:20 NRSV

The space was dark, the cliffs reached up and up with a slice of light only, and that was scores of feet overhead. We were in Jordan, riding into Petra on horseback. The rocky gorge was so narrow there were times when I could touch the rocks on either side. On we rode, until at last we emerged into a valley filled with light. A columned temple carved into rock towered ahead of us. We saw hundreds of homes dug deep into stone. There were the ruins of a theater, a marketplace and a water system. The only entrance to the rock-surrounded valley was the worm-like gorge. Enemies would be forced to access the city one at a time. So this, I thought, is what it means for God to be our refuge—hidden from sight, sheltered from all enemies, safe.

GROUP DISCUSSION. From what kinds of pressures or problems do you sometimes feel you need a refuge?

PERSONAL REFLECTION. What experiences or places come to mind when you think of a safe place to hide?

What kinds of situations make you want to run to such a place so you can find comfort and perspective?

David's Psalm 31 is a song written after a profound experience of God's fortressing. It is a challenge to stand on the fact of the reliable shelter God promises to be for us, even when, and especially when, we are "going to pieces." *Read Psalm 31.*

1. What can you tell about David's frame of mind from these verses?

When have you felt like this?

2. List the different phrases David uses to explain God as a refuge.

3. Note David's emotional and intellectual progression in verses 1-5. Why does he speak of his spirit in verse 5?

4. What past, present and future events does David refer to in verses 6-8?

_____

5. Study David's habits of prayer in verses 3, 5, 7-8 especially. What patterns do you see that you would like to incorporate in your own prayer life?

_____

6. We commit idolatry (v. 6) when we refuse to admit our inherent need for God and try to satisfy this need with something else. Idolatry manifests itself in over-attachment or over-investment. What are some of the idols we worship today?

_____

7. What are the specific reasons for David's distress (vv. 9-13)?

How is David's emotional trauma affecting his body?

_____

8. Why do you think David alludes to himself as "broken pottery" in verse 12?

_____

9. We may not be able to identify with the wars that were a major part of David's life, but we can identify with the wounds of rejection. What past or present wounds or injustices are you dealing with?

---

10. Look at verses 14-18. The word *times* carries the meaning of "appointment" or "course of life." How can the truth of verse 15 provide a shelter in uncertain circumstances?

---

11. In two columns record what is visible and what is invisible according to verses 19-24. List first the visible and then the invisible acts or states of both God and man.

What insight did you gain from this exercise?

---

12. If we seek to probe the vastness of God, we will need to be honest about the negatives of life. We will also need to be alert to the daily signs of his love, however, and the goodnesses that are there (v. 19). "I find I can't live without hope," said Madeleine L' Engle (in *Victoria*). "Good things happen that we can't believe." What goodnesses do you believe God is storing up for you as you take refuge in him?

Thank the Lord for how he has protected you in the past, how he's protecting you now and how he will protect you in the future.

Now or Later

Responding with Praise. Read or sing the following hymn.

A Mighty Fortress

A mighty fortress is our God,
A bulwark never failing;
Our helper He, amid the flood
Of mortal ills prevailing:
For still our ancient foe
Doth seek to work us woe;
His craft and power are great,
And, armed with cruel hate,
On earth is not his equal. . . .

That word above all earthly powers,
No thanks to them, abideth;
The Spirit and the gifts are ours
Through him who with us sideth:
Let goods and kindred go,
This mortal life also;
The body they may kill:
God's truth abideth still;
His kingdom is forever.

Martin Luther

Worship Journal. God is with us when we walk down a crowded street, but he is normally crammed into a tiny nook of our consciousness. If we take the time to seek him in a quiet place, we become more aware of him. When it is time then to return to the street, we carry him larger within us, finding it easier to take refuge in him even in the crowd. Write about why it is difficult to set aside leisurely time with God. What will you do about it?

9

The God Who Loves

Psalm 36

How priceless is your unfailing love!
PSALM 36:7

The biblical writers speak of God's love from different angles. Hosea tells of the God who is a faithful husband despite his spouse's unfaithfulness. Solomon reveals God as a bridegroom who delights in beautiful intimacy with his bride, praising her as priceless. The gospel writers describe the love of Christ, a friend and brother who sealed his love with the sacrifice of his life.

The psalmists stitch the silken thread of God's love through the majority of the psalms. They mention it in the course of praising, pleading, wondering, laughing, needing, fearing, rejoicing, complaining and contemplating. They speak of God as a compassionate Father, as King/Messiah, whose bride awaits him "all glorious . . . within her chamber" (Psalm 45:13). God is Champion, whose "steadfast love endures forever" (Psalm 136 RSV). And God is Maker, who protects and woos the thing he has made.

GROUP DISCUSSION. Discuss the different kinds of love we experience. Consider, for example, how a mother's love is different from a friend's love; a friend's love from a sweetheart's love; a father's love from a mother's love.

PERSONAL REFLECTION. What kind of love appeals to you the most right now? Why do you think you feel this way at this point in your life?

God's love is a synergism of all the loves we give and receive. God is father, mother, creator, lover, brother, sister and friend. His godliness and our creatureliness dictate a gap of understanding. In Psalm 36, sometimes soaring but always practical, David explores what we need to understand about God's love to help us survive the difficulties of our relationships. *Read Psalm 36.*

---

1. How would you summarize or title each section of this psalm?

Verses 1-4:

Verses 5-9:

Verses 10-12:

---

2. Why do you think David begins with a meditation on why trouble-makers do what they do and then turns so abruptly to a contemplation of God's love? (Consider what you know about the events of David's life.)

---

3. When is it difficult for you to understand human wickness? (Cite an example, if you can, without undermining a particular individual.)

What insight (oracle) has David been given about why people turn to wickedness (vv. 1-4)?

___

4. The thoroughness of God's love reveals itself even more clearly when we set it beside the faithlessness of humanity. Read verses 5-9 again. What words or phrases tell us something about God's love and how it manifests itself?

___

5. Why do you think the psalmist compared God's love to something that seemed limitless and his righteousness to something limited (vv. 5-7)?

___

6. Verse 6 says that God "preserves" us. Think about what it means to preserve something (for example, an old book, fruit or a friendship). How does this enlarge your understanding of what God does for us out of Creator-love?

___

7. Meditate for a moment on verse 7, picturing yourself in the scene described. How does the idea of God giving you refuge under the shadow of his wings affect you personally?

8. Note David's description of feasting in verse 8. What kinds of feelings or thoughts do you have toward a person you are willing to go to a lot of trouble for or entertain lavishly?

---

9. Reread verses 9-11. Our divine lover wants to give us lives characterized by vigor, clarity and security. Which of these three manifestations of God's love do you particularly need right now? Explain.

---

10. What aspect of love is the psalmist asking to see in verses 10-12?

---

11. Knowing God on a daily basis has to do with recognition, recognition of answers to prayer and of other events in which he has had a hand. What have you experienced recently that reassures you that God is with you and that he loves you?

Praise God, your father and maker; Jesus, your friend, brother and lover; and the Holy Spirit, your comforter and guide, for their immeasurable love. Ask God to help you recognize that love in your life.

Now or Later

Responding with Praise. Read or sing the following hymn.

The Love of God

Could we with ink the ocean fill,
And were the skies of parchment made,
Were every stalk on earth a quill,
And every man a scribe by trade,
To write the love of God above,
Would drain the ocean dry.

Nor could the scroll contain the whole,
Though stretched from sky to sky.
O love of God, how rich and pure!
How measureless and strong
It shall for evermore endure
The saints and angel's song.

F. M. Lehman

Worship Journal. Consider James 4:6-8 (*The Message*): "What he gives in love is far better than anything else you'll find. . . . Say a quiet yes to God, and he'll be there in no time." Write a poem or a meditation about how you have experienced God's love as the best love.

10

The God Who Reigns

Psalm 145

My mouth will speak in praise of the LORD.
Let every creature praise his holy name
for ever and ever.
PSALM 145:21

God's kingdom includes the kind of power demonstrated in a volcano erupting or an earthquake destroying a city. He's the king whose eyes are like flames of fire, whose mouth wields a two-edged sword. Someday we will be able to look at such glory and have no need to tremble, but now we beg a more tender God. If we dwell too long on his dangerous omnipotence, we will only become more fearful.

Life is a fearful affair. Our technology solves surface problems, but root problems remain, emerging in psychological disease. Our only hope is the fact that God is not only fiercely powerful but also fiercely loving and good.

GROUP DISCUSSION. Name some earthly kings or leaders (or perhaps an authority figure in your own life) who wielded their power for good. How did they demonstrate concern for people under them?

PERSONAL REFLECTION. How do you feel about authority?

What negative or positive experiences have caused you to feel this way?

God is the ultimate authority and deserves our praise. C. S. Lewis said, "All enjoyment spontaneously overflows into praise" (*Reflections on the Psalms*). Psalm 145 gives us more reasons to praise. *Read Psalm 145.*

1. Why is David praising God in this psalm? List as many reasons as you can find.

2. Notice the emphasis of verses 1-2 and verse 21. David brings his relationship with the King of kings down to the everyday. He makes a vow not to pass even one day of his life without praising God for something. What would you like to praise God for today?

3. Review verses 3-7. What words here help you picture David's response to God's greatness? Why?

4. The New American Standard Bible translates verse 7, "They shall eagerly utter the memory of Thine abundant goodness and shall shout joyfully of Thy righteousness." When have you found yourself "shouting" about God's righteousness?

When are you likely to resist shouting about your experience of God?

5. Read verses 8-20 a second time. What phrases do you see that include the word *all?*

Taken as a whole, what do these phrases reveal about God?

6. Why do you think the verses on God's kingdom and glory (vv. 11-13) are sandwiched in between specifics about his deeds of love? (Consider different connotations of the word *glory*.)

7. What conditions do you have to fill to become a candidate for tenderness from the King of kings (vv. 9, 14-15, 16-18)?

8. The Living Bible translates verse 14, "The Lord lifts the fallen and those bent beneath their loads." In what area of your life do you feel the need to be lifted, braced or given a place to lean?

9. Verses 15, 18 and 19 give us several principles about prayer. What stands out to you?

10. The infinite glory of God's rule lies above all in the tenderness and compassion he bestows on his subjects. He is the king of love, and we will never run out of reasons to praise him. What changes would you like to make in your prayer life as a result of studying this psalm?

Ask the Lord to give you eyes to see his daily wonders, to grant you a heart of praise.

Now or Later

Responding with Praise. Read or sing the following hymn.

Blessed Be the Lord God Almighty

Father in heaven, how we love You,
We lift Your name in all the earth.
May Your Kingdom be established in our praises
As Your people declare Your mighty works.
Blessed be the Lord God Almighty,
Who was, and is, and is to come.
Blessed be the Lord God Almighty,
Who reigns forever more.

By Bob Fitts ©1984 Scripture in Song (Administered by Maranatha! Music c/o The Copyright Company, Nashville, TN). Used by permission.

Worship Journal. God is always near. Realizing this opens up his majesty, his power in simple things. A drop of water can be as powerful as a volcano. Make a list of different glories in the world that are "small," and use them for a time of praise.

At the end of your worship time, decide on a long-term plan for working in your worship journal (perhaps once a week). Some ideas: review the psalms in this book, or read more of the psalms; use a hymnbook to worship; memorize and meditate on meaningful promises from Scripture.

Leader's Notes

MY GRACE IS SUFFICIENT FOR YOU. (2 COR 12:9)

Leading a Bible discussion can be an enjoyable and rewarding experience. But it can also be *scary*—especially if you've never done it before. If this is your feeling, you're in good company. When God asked Moses to lead the Israelites out of Egypt, he replied, "O Lord, please send someone else to do it!" (Ex 4:13). It was the same with Solomon, Jeremiah and Timothy, but God helped these people in spite of their weaknesses, and he will help you as well.

You don't need to be an expert on the Bible or a trained teacher to lead a Bible discussion. The idea behind these inductive studies is that the leader guides group members to discover for themselves what the Bible has to say. This method of learning will allow group members to remember much more of what is said than a lecture would.

These studies are designed to be led easily. As a matter of fact, the flow of questions through the passage from observation to interpretation to application is so natural that you may feel that the studies lead themselves. This study guide is also flexible. You can use it with a variety of groups—student, professional, neighborhood or church groups. Each study takes forty-five to sixty minutes in a group setting.

There are some important facts to know about group dynamics and encouraging discussion. The suggestions listed below should enable you to effectively and enjoyably fulfill your role as leader.

Preparing for the Study

1. Ask God to help you understand and apply the passage in your own life. Unless this happens, you will not be prepared to lead others. Pray too for the various members of the group. Ask God to open your hearts to the message of his Word and motivate you to action.

2. Read the introduction to the entire guide to get an overview of the entire book and the issues which will be explored.

3. As you begin each study, read and reread the assigned Bible passage to familiarize yourself with it.

4. This study guide is based on the New International Version of the Bible. It will help you and the group if you use this translation as the basis for your study and discussion.

5. Carefully work through each question in the study. Spend time in meditation and reflection as you consider how to respond.

6. Write your thoughts and responses in the space provided in the study guide. This will help you to express your understanding of the passage clearly.

7. It might help to have a Bible dictionary handy. Use it to look up any unfamiliar words, names or places. (For additional help on how to study a passage, see chapter five of *How to Lead a LifeGuide Bible Study,* InterVarsity Press.)

8. Consider how you can apply the Scripture to your life. Remember that the group will follow your lead in responding to the studies. They will not go any deeper than you do.

9. Once you have finished your own study of the passage, familiarize yourself with the leader's notes for the study you are leading. These are designed to help you in several ways. First, they tell you the purpose the study guide author had in mind when writing the study. Take time to think through how the study questions work together to accomplish that purpose. Second, the notes provide you with additional background information or suggestions on group dynamics for various questions. This information can be useful when people have difficulty understanding or answering a question. Third, the leader's notes can alert you to potential problems you may encounter during the study.

10. If you wish to remind yourself of anything mentioned in the leader's notes, make a note to yourself below that question in the study.

Leading the Study

1. Begin the study on time. Open with prayer, asking God to help the group to understand and apply the passage.

2. Be sure that everyone in your group has a study guide. Encourage the group to prepare beforehand for each discussion by reading the introduction to the guide and by working through the questions in the study.

3. At the beginning of your first time together, explain that these studies are meant to be discussions, not lectures. Encourage the members of the group to participate. However, do not put pressure on those who may be hesitant to speak during the first few sessions. You may want to suggest the following guidelines to your group.

☐ Stick to the topic being discussed.

☐ Your responses should be based on the verses which are the focus of the discussion and not on outside authorities such as commentaries or speakers.

☐ These studies focus on a particular passage of Scripture. Only rarely should you refer to other portions of the Bible. This allows for everyone to participate in in-depth study on equal ground.

☐ Anything said in the group is considered confidential and will not be discussed outside the group unless specific permission is given to do so.

☐ We will listen attentively to each other and provide time for each person present to talk.

☐ We will pray for each other.

4. Have a group member read the introduction at the beginning of the discussion.

5. Every session begins with a group discussion question. The question or activity is meant to be used before the passage is read. The question introduces the theme of the study and encourages group members to begin to open up. Encourage as many members as possible to participate, and be ready to get the discussion going with your own response.

This section is designed to reveal where our thoughts or feelings need to be transformed by Scripture. That is why it is especially important not to read the passage before the discussion question is asked. The passage will tend to color the honest reactions people would otherwise give because they are, of course, supposed to think the way the Bible does.

You may want to supplement the group discussion question with an icebreaker to help people to get comfortable. See the community section of *Small Group Idea Book* for more ideas.

You also might want to use the personal reflection question with your group. Either allow a time of silence for people to respond individually or discuss it together.

6. Have a group member (or members if the passage is long) read aloud the passage to be studied. Then give people several minutes to read the passage again silently so that they can take it all in.

7. Question 1 will generally be an overview question designed to briefly survey the passage. Encourage the group to look at the whole passage, but try to avoid getting sidetracked by questions or issues that will be addressed later in the study.

8. As you ask the questions, keep in mind that they are designed to be used just as they are written. You may simply read them aloud. Or you may prefer to express them in your own words.

There may be times when it is appropriate to deviate from the study guide. For example, a question may have already been answered. If so, move on to the next question. Or someone may raise an important question not covered in the guide. Take time to discuss it, but try to keep the group from going off on tangents.

9. Avoid answering your own questions. If necessary, repeat or rephrase them until they are clearly understood. Or point out something you read in the leader's notes to clarify the context or meaning. An eager group quickly becomes passive and silent if they think the leader will do most of the talking.

10. Don't be afraid of silence. People may need time to think about the question before formulating their answers.

11. Don't be content with just one answer. Ask, "What do the rest of you think?" or "Anything else?" until several people have given answers to the question.

12. Acknowledge all contributions. Try to be affirming whenever possible. Never reject an answer. If it is clearly off-base, ask, "Which verse led you to that conclusion?" or again, "What do the rest of you think?"

13. Don't expect every answer to be addressed to you, even though this will probably happen at first. As group members become more at ease, they will begin to truly interact with each other. This is one sign of healthy discussion.

14. Don't be afraid of controversy. It can be very stimulating. If you don't resolve an issue completely, don't be frustrated. Move on and keep it in mind for later. A subsequent study may solve the problem.

15. Periodically summarize what the group has said about the passage. This helps to draw together the various ideas mentioned and gives continuity to the study. But don't preach.

16. At the end of the Bible discussion you may want to allow group members a time of quiet to work on an idea under "Now or Later." Then discuss what you experienced. Or you may want to encourage group members to work on these ideas between meetings. Give an opportunity during the session for people to talk about what they are learning.

17. Conclude your time together with conversational prayer, adapting the prayer suggestion at the end of the study to your group. Ask for God's help in following through on the commitments you've made.

18. End on time.

Many more suggestions and helps are found in *How to Lead a LifeGuide Bible Study.*

Components of Small Groups

A healthy small group should do more than study the Bible. There are four components to consider as you structure your time together.

Nurture. Small groups help us to grow in our knowledge and love of God. Bible study is the key to making this happen and is the foundation of your small group.

Community. Small groups are a great place to develop deep friendships with other Christians. Allow time for informal interaction before and after each study. Plan activities and games that will help you get to know each other. Spend time having fun together—going on a picnic or cooking dinner together.

Worship and prayer. Your study will be enhanced by spending time praising God together in prayer or song. Pray for each other's needs—and keep track of how God is answering prayer in your group. Ask God to help you to apply what you are learning in your study.

Outreach. Reaching out to others can be a practical way of applying what you are learning, and it will keep your group from becoming self-focused. Host a series of evangelistic discussions for your friends or neighbors. Clean up the yard of an elderly friend. Serve at a soup kitchen together, or spend a day working on a Habitat house.

Many more suggestions and helps in each of these areas are found in *Small Group Idea Book.* Information on building a small group can be found in *Small Group Leaders' Handbook* and *The Big Book on Small Groups* (both from Inter-Varsity Press). Reading through one of these books would be worth your time.

Study 1. The God Who Satisfies. Psalm 104.

Purpose: To praise God for his daily provision and trust him for future satisfaction.

Group discussion. Every study begins with an approach question, which is meant to be asked before the passage is read. These questions are important for several reasons.

First, the group discussion question helps the group to warm up to each other. No matter how well a group may know each other, there is always a stiffness that needs to be overcome before people will begin to talk openly. A good question will break the ice.

Second, approach questions get people thinking along the lines of the topic of the study. Most people will have lots of different things going on in their minds (dinner, an important meeting coming up, how to get the car fixed) that will have nothing to do with the study. A creative question will get their attention and draw them into the discussion.

Third, approach questions can reveal where our thoughts or feelings need to be transformed by Scripture. Giving honest responses before they find out what the Bible says may help them see where their thoughts or attitudes need to be changed.

In the group discussion encourage as much fun, light sharing as you can. This question should be nonthreatening.

Personal reflection. This question is designed to open the themes of the session for individuals studying on their own. If you are studying in a group, you could also use this question. Allow group members five minutes of quiet to complete this exercise, and then briefly discuss what you experienced.

General note. Concerning the authorship of this psalm and the rest of the psalms in this book, Henry Halley says that although David is considered the principal author of the psalms, "The Titles are not a certain indication of Authorship; for 'of' 'to,' and 'for,' are the same preposition in Hebrew. A Psalm 'of' David may have been one that he himself wrote, or that was written 'for' David, or dedicated 'to' David."

Halley goes on to say that in some cases anonymous psalms are attributed to the person who authored the preceding psalm. David is thought to be the author of some of these psalms (*Halley's Bible Handbook*).

Question 1. This question is an overview question. Guide the group quickly through the whole psalm, encouraging them to mention any themes they see.

Question 2. At some point in your discussion of images, explain that the chief formal characteristic of Hebrew poetry is parallelism, the practice of saying the same thing twice in different words. You may also want to discuss the definitions of other kinds of images used in poetry. A simile is a figure of speech in which one thing is likened to another, dissimilar thing by the use of "like" or "as." A metaphor is a figure of speech containing an implied comparison, in which a word or phrase ordinarily and primarily used of one thing is applied to another. Personification is a figure of speech in which a thing, quality or idea is represented as a person.

Question 3. If you need to jog the group's thinking, mention that from verse 7 you learn that when God speaks, things happen. Then ask, "What do you learn about him from verses 8-9?"

Question 4. Optional follow-up question: Since God is love, what kind of boundaries do you think he sets to help his people during difficult times?

Question 5. Your group may decide on universal needs, such as the quenching of thirsts, the provision of homes or security, the provision of order and the gift of variety. Note how he cares for people, especially in verse 15.

Question 7. In preparation for questions about Psalm 104:29, consider the following: Death and suffering are the consequences of our sin. God, as a loving redeemer, can and does bring ultimate good from both.

Question 9. If your group has already established a level of trust, invite anyone who desires to do so to express aloud what they have written.

Responding with Praise. A study of the psalms is not complete without some form of singing. If you are studying with a group, see if you can find a guitarist, pianist or singer who is willing to lead a short time of singing at the end of each study. Suggested songs are a part of each chapter.

Worship Journal. Encourage group members to keep extra paper or a notebook with their study book so they can use these exercises to go deeper. There are several ways to do this: (1) instruct group members to complete this first session before the study, (2) begin completing them this week and ask for insights next week, or (3) allow ten or fifteen minutes of quiet at the beginning or end of the group for people to journal. Each week, before you close with the song, ask if anyone would like to talk about what they have learned and experienced. Make these insights part of your prayer and praise.

Study 2. The God Who Understands. Psalm 147.
Purpose: To praise God for his hand in the mysterious visible and invisible world.
Group discussion. God is the source of everything good. Think of the rain that silvers the streets, the peace that comes almost touchable in a moment of prayer, the latest galactic discovery and the growing reverence in the heart of the scientist. The macrocosm and the microcosm live and maintain their living because of God.
Question 1. You may want to add the following application question to your discussion: What does the fact that all the verbs about God are present tense say to you?
Question 5. If the group needs more guidance, ask the following questions: What inward, invisible things does God value? Why is he contrasting verse 10 with verse 11? If necessary, use 1 Samuel 16:1-7 to shed light on verses 10-11. God values the invisible attitudes of the heart, such as trust and humility, more than any show of power.
You may need to discuss what it means to "fear God." As applied to the relationship between God and the believer it means to have "a reverential fear . . . as a controlling motive of the life . . . not a mere fear of His power and righteous retribution, but a wholesome dread of displeasing Him." This kind of reverential fear is the result of loving him and desiring to honor him with our lives (W. E. Vine, *An Expository Dictionary of New Testament Words* [Nashville: Thomas Nelson, 1981]).
Question 6. If there are questions about God's provision, you may want to introduce the following thoughts about God's unfailing goodness. The psalmist speaks of young ravens in verse 9, but not every raven finds food in every instance, just as not all our prayers are answered in the time we desire. But overall, when we consider the entire lifeline of the earth, of humankind, of our families and descendants, God does provide. His plan is to heal permanently. Romans 8:18-23 shows us that creation groans in this age but that we are moving inexorably toward wholeness and peace.
Question 7. To make this more personal, remember that life is often a battle. If you want to spend more time on the personal aspect of God's strengthening, ask the following: "How is God a refuge, a fortress to us personally?" You may want to stop at this point and use verses 12-14 to pray for your nation.
Question 9. Read Isaiah 55:10-11 to better understand this concept of God's Word being alive. You may need to explain that the words *commands, laws* and *decrees* (sometimes translated "precepts") are often used as synonyms for God's Word.

Study 3. The God Who Helps. Psalm 40.
Purpose: To realize that no one is completely self-sufficient and to understand

more about God's desire to help us.

Question 1. It will help if you make a list ahead of time including attitudes and events to which David refers that are in the past, present and future. You may also want to list any principles you notice. This should involve the group with every verse of the psalm.

Question 2. For more discussion, ask the group, "What would enable you to wait patiently in that situation?"

Question 4. The Berkely translation of verse 5 says, "You have made numerous your thoughts toward us." If someone asks the meaning of verse 4, you can use Psalm 146:3 as a cross reference, which says, "Do not put your trust in princes, in mortal men, who cannot save." The counsel of those who trust in false gods (such as money, pleasure or human reasoning) will often prevent us from receiving the blessings God would give us.

Question 6. After reading the Hebrews passage, you could ask, "What is the source of goodness?" Also, note in verse 6 that the phrase "My ears you have pierced" was David's "recognition that God had given him the ability to hear and obey the Word of the Lord"(John F. Walvoord and Roy B. Zuck, eds., *The Bible Knowledge Commentary* [Wheaton, Ill.: Victor, 1983-1985]).

Note on Old Testament sacrifices: "The Old Testament law prescribed five kinds of sacrifices; the burnt-offering, the meat-offering, . . . the peace-offering, . . . the sin-offering and the trespass offering. . . . There was first a sin-offering, as an approach to God; next a burnt-offering, typical of dedication to His service" (William Smith, *Smith's Bible Dictionary* [Westwood, N.J.: Barbour, 1987]).

Question 8. Note the use of the word *your.*

Question 10. C. S. Lewis shed some insight on David's vengeful prayer in verses 14-15 when he said that some of David's psalms express "a feeling we all know only too well, resentment, expressing itself with perfect freedom, without shame—as few but children would express it today." The restraints in the ancient Hebrew culture were different from ours. Theirs was "a world of savage punishments. We are far more subtle than they in disguising our ill will from others and from ourselves" (C. S. Lewis, *Reflections on the Psalms* [New York: Harcourt, Brace, 1958]).

If there is time, ask the following question before question 11: "David was a warrior of unprecedented bravery, a military genius and a brilliant statesman. After studying this psalm how do you feel about the importance of being self-sufficient?"

Study 4. The God Who Calms Fears. Psalm 27.

Purpose: To grow in the ability to trust God with personal worries and fears.

Question 1. Optional follow-up question: What do we learn about David's problems?

Question 3. Other psalms broaden the concept of God's being a stronghold

by using such words as *refuge, fortress, place of safety, defense, rock, strength.*
Modern equivalents would be "an army that defends," "a place to rest from
overwork," "a place to hide from verbal attacks or demands," "a shelter in a
blizzard."

Question 4. Encourage the group to think about unseen enemies—enemies
from within as well as from without. (Make your own list ahead of time.)

Question 5. If you have non-Christians in your group, you may want to use
the following question: "How does a person go about seeking God?"

Question 6. If your group needs a follow-up question, try, "What do you
think of as a time or place of personal refuge?"

Question 7. Appropriate titles or themes might include verse 7, "Plea for
Mercy"; verse 8, "Reminding God of Obedience"; verse 9, "Being Honest
About Doubts or Remembering God's Past Help"; verse 10, "Claiming a
Promise"; verse 11, "Teach Me, Lord"; verse 12, "Save Me from My Enemies."

Question 10. Optional follow-up questions: What is David waiting for? In
what situations do you find it difficult to wait?

Question 11. Conclude this time of sharing what God has done by having a
short time of prayer. Suggest including praise and petitions about areas of
current worry.

Study 5. The God Who Restores. Psalm 30.
Purpose: To begin to trust God's mercy in difficult times.

Question 1. Have the group read the psalm antiphonally to experience how
David may have had it performed. Verses 1-3: leader; verses 4-5: all; verses
6-10: leader; verses 11-12: all.

Question 2. A review of Solomon's dedication of the temple reveals that ded-
ications included the blowing of trumpets, feasting, sacrifices, petitions,
music and praises for God's acts of faithfulness.

Question 3. The Hebrew word for depths is "Sheol, the abode of the dead." It
is "the place of gloom and decay" (Allen C. Myers, ed., *Eerdman's Bible
Dictionary* [Grand Rapids: Eerdmans, 1987]).

Question 4. The use of the word *healed* is not limited to physical illness in
the Bible. Psalm 41:4, for example, speaks of being healed from sin. Affliction
also is often described as a disease.

Question 5. Notice that David is addressing "saints." Discuss the idea of
favor as compared to mercy. When someone in the Bible is described as
receiving favor, the gifts are lavish. Noah finds favor in God's eyes and
becomes the patriarch of a new world. Joseph finds favor in Potiphar's eyes
and is awarded a high position in the official's household. Ruth finds favor in
Boaz's eyes and is provided abundantly with food and work. Esther receives
favor from the king and becomes the queen.

Question 7. Encourage people to share their experiences of a father-figure and how those experiences affect their view of God today. In Hebrew, God's anger is expressed in very human, emotional terms. His nostrils flare. His anger burns. But he is slow to anger, and the Bible indicates he is most apt to be angry in extreme situations. One example is before the flood, when God said, "Every inclination of the thoughts of his heart was only evil all the time" (Gen 6:5). God also hates pride (Prov 16:5). We invite God's wrath when we exalt ourselves instead of God.

Question 8. In your personal study, you may want to reread Psalm 30 and note other cases when the second phrase sheds further light. The poetic image of God's "hiding his face" symbolizes broken communion. When he doesn't hide his face, there is beautiful and open communion. One scholar says, "In his self-complacent elation [perhaps his recent access to the throne] David was checked by God's hiding His face" (J. D. Douglas, ed., *New Commentary on the Whole Bible* [Wheaton, Ill.: Tyndale House, 1990]).

Question 12. You may want to review the fact here that God's lasting favor is directed toward the people who belong to him—saints. Saints are people who are objects of God's lovingkindness (*hesed*). Old Testament scholar R. Laird Harris says, *hesed*, "as used in the Old Testament is love with forgiveness, mercy with pardon. It denotes free acts of rescue or deliverance" (R. Laird Harris, Gleason L. Archer Jr. and Bruce K. Waltke, eds., *Theological Wordbook of the Old Testament* [Chicago: Moody Press, 1980]).

Study 6. The God Who Strengthens. Psalm 18:1-36.
Purpose: To encourage faith in God's provision of strength for every difficulty.
Group discussion. Guide the group in exploring all kinds of strength: strength of character, will, stamina and so on.

Question 1. The word *strength* in verse 1 comes from a Hebrew root which means "to be or grow firm or strong" (Robert L. Thomas, ed., *New American Standard Exhaustive Concordance of the Bible* [Anaheim, Calif.: Foundation Publications, 1998]). You may want to explore the different kinds of strength imaged in words like *rock, fortress* and *shield*. "The horn, as the means of attack or defense of some of the strongest animals, is a frequent emblem of power or strength efficiently exercised" (*New Commentary on the Whole Bible*). A stronghold is a secure height.

Question 2. This is a very personal psalm in which David reviews the many ways God has strengthened and delivered him in the past. Read 1 Samuel 30:1-25 to learn about one specific situation when God rode the heavens to David's help.

Question 5. To help the group understand why David is using the kind of imagery he is in this section, share the fact that, "God's coming [is] described in figures drawn from His appearance on Sinai" (*New Commentary on the Whole Bible*).

Question 7. David is most likely referring to his official conduct and purposes during different wars in which he defended God's people.

Question 10. You may want to facilitate the discussion by preparing a list of ways that God has trained you for an unexpected challenge by encouraging your growth in some attitude or skill. If time allows, you may want to read verses 37-50. After David finishes his tales of victory in verses 37-45, he sings a doxology to God (vv. 46-50). Ask the group, "Why is the phrase 'The Lord lives' (v. 46) especially poignant at the end of this psalm?"

Study 7. The God Who Listens. Psalm 34.

Purpose: To increase our awareness of God's attentiveness and his desire for ours.

Question 2. David is encouraging readers to see the Lord as greater than they realize—greater in attentiveness, devotion and thoughtfulness. He wants them to allow God to increase in size and importance in their lives.

Question 4. The word *shame* in verse 5 refers to the "loss of self possession through humiliation, embarrassment or confusion" (*Theological Wordbook*). David used questionable means to extricate himself from a dangerous circumstance. He pretended he was insane. Ingenious this might have been, but David takes no glory in it. He calls himself a "poor man" and gives God all the credit for his deliverance from Abimelech.

The angel of the Lord is sometimes distinguished from God. Other times they are the same. Matthew Henry describes the angel of verse 7 as a lifeguard or guard of angels that minister to those who bear his image.

Question 5. God sometimes meets our needs by giving us ideas or directing us to take specific steps. You may want to allow time now for people to pray about the needs mentioned. Have them spend five to eight minutes listening to God and writing down their impressions. Then you might want to discuss them. You might prefer to do this at the end of the study or simply direct people to try it between studies.

Question 6. You may want to guide the group in a discussion of the idea of tasting God. How might your experience of God's goodness be like the taste of a favorite dish? When have you experienced God's sweetness or tenderness or, perhaps, the warmth of his presence in a cold circumstance?

Question 7. You might wonder if your sins could cause God to "cut off [your] memory" from the earth (v. 16). Eugene Peterson describes an evil person as one "who makes a practice of doing evil, addicted to denial and illusion" (John 3:19 *The Message*). This implies a person who is entrenched in rebellion, not a believer who occasionally slips.

Question 8. James 3:2, 6 is an excellent commentary on the pivotal place of the tongue in a believer's life.

Question 9. The Hebrew word for *pursue* means "to chase or persecute." The "term usually refers to a man or group pursuing another for purpose of making war or taking revenge" (*Theological Wordbook*). Instead of chasing after someone who has wrongly used us in order to wreak vengeance, we are to zealously track them down in order to restore harmony.

Study 8. The God Who Gives Refuge. Psalm 31.
Purpose: To begin to understand and experience God as our most reliable refuge.
Group discussion. If the group has difficulty responding, tell them about a need in your own life. This will encourage them to be open.
Question 2. The word *refuge* has the basic meaning of security.
Question 3. In verse 5, David is praying for the protection at least of his soul. "If my time has come," he says, "it is well with my soul."
Question 5. The prayer disciplines David demonstrates are (1) a thankful heart, remembering past interventions and blessings, (2) a praying heart, naming specific fears, (3) an expectant heart, expectantly claiming God's promises and (4) a believing heart, praising God for what he is going to do.
Question 6. Consider that our tendency is to worship what gives us a sense of control. At this point you may want to stop and ask people to pinpoint the idol they tend to rely on. Then take time to pray or write a confession to God. If needed, refer to the leader's note for study 3, question 10 for C. S. Lewis's explanation of David's vengeful prayers.
Question 8. See also Jeremiah 18:5-6 and Isaiah 30:13-14.
Question 9. If someone feels that they aren't dealing with any wounds, then they might reflect on the wounds of a close friend or relative. You may want to read this excerpt from Robert Browning's poem *Rabbi Ben Ezra*, "Our times are in His hand Who saith, 'A whole I planned,' Youth shows but half; trust God: see all, nor be afraid. . . . Maker, remake, complete—I trust what Thou shalt do!" (George Herbert, *Selections from Browning*).
Question 11. You may want to point out the fact that David anchors his poem in three places with the pivotal importance of trust—verses 6, 15 and 24. Every time we choose to place our trust in God instead of a favorite idol, we give God an opportunity to strengthen our faith and our hope for the future.

Study 9. The God Who Loves. Psalm 36.
Purpose: To enlarge the group's understanding of the exhaustive nature of God's love.
Question 1. Possible titles for the sections: (a) A New Truth: The Proud One's Heart Is Full of Destructive Evil; (b) An Old Truth: God's Heart Is Abundant in Need-Meeting Love; (c) A Prayer: In Your Love Protect Us Against the Evil! Or (a) The Reason Human Love Fails; (b) Assurances God's Love Won't Fail; (c) Knowing (or Experiencing) God's Love.

Question 2. If your group needs some help with this question, have them review verses 10-11. When you think of the psalm as a whole, keeping the first four verses in context and considering David's history of friends and family turning against him, David seems to have asked God for insight into the question, "Why have people who loved me turned against me in unbelievable wickedness?" He then turns to the stability of God's love. See 1 Samuel 18:1-11 and 2 Samuel 15:1-21 concerning David's relationship with King Saul and with his own son Absalom for more information.

Question 3. For more understanding of the pathos of a self-centered life versus a God-centered life, compare the mood of verse 4 to the mood of verses 8-9.

Question 5. Your group will probably observe that when we consider our own failings, we all feel more need for someone's love than we do for someone's justice or righteousness. This psalm suggests that God's love is more expansive than his justice. "When it's sin versus grace, grace wins hands-down" (Rom 5:20 *The Message*).

Question 8. You may also want to read Song of Solomon 2:1-5 for another picture of feasting.

Question 9. C. S. Lewis says God's love "is a love that has no hunger that needs to be filled, only plenteousness that desires to give" (*The Four Loves* [New York: Harcourt Brace Jovanovich, 1991]).

Study 10. The God Who Reigns. Psalm 145.
Purpose: To encourage the group to make a new commitment to praise and prayer.

General note. If you feel it is appropriate for your group, make this last study special by bringing a recording of Beethoven's 9th Symphony. Play the last movement ("Ode to Joy") during your study.

Group discussion. Be especially sensitive to where the Spirit seems to be leading your discussion during this last hour together. It may be more important to listen to each other than to cover all the material.

Question 2. Extend this time, encouraging people to share any positive thing that has happened in the last week or two.

Question 4. Remind the group that an important part of David's prayer life was reviewing what God had done for him in the past. A prayer journal is a helpful tool for reviewing answered prayers. You may also want to use this guiding question: What doubts keep us from celebrating his abundant goodness?

Question 6. A reasonable response to God's glory is fear. We may want to distance ourselves from God, who is so far above us. Yet God's love invites us to draw near and enjoy his presence.

Question 7. If discussion lags, use the following as true/false questions. God is tender only (1) toward those who keep most of his laws; (2) toward those who believe he exists; (3) toward all who have needs; (4) toward those who have the right amount of faith; (5) toward those who aren't extremely wicked; (6) toward every creature he has made.

God expresses his unconditional love toward the believer in Hebrews 13:5: "Never will I leave you, never will I forsake you." Amy Carmichael says, "Westcott interprets this verse, 'I will in no wise desert you or leave you alone in the field of contest, or in a position of suffering; I will in no wise let go— loose hold—my sustaining grasp' " (Amy Carmichael, *Edges of His Ways*).

Question 8. People in your group will be experiencing anxieties, defeats, rejections, physical problems, financial difficulties, temptations and other hardships. Take a few minutes to pray for these needs. Close the prayer time by reading verse 21 aloud together.

Ruth Ann Ridley is a freelance writer who has led Bible studies for over thirty years. She has a degree in piano performance and currently serves with her husband on the associate staff of the Navigators. The author of the Women of Character Bible Study Series *(NavPress) and* Every Marriage Is Different *(Victor Books), she has also written a historical novel on the life of J. S. Bach (Sebastian, Quiddity Press).*